AWESOME ATHLETES

TIGER WOODS

Paul Joseph

ABDO & Daughters

visit us at
www.abdopub.com

Published by Abdo & Daughters, 4940 Viking Drive, Suite 622, Edina, Minnesota 55435.

Copyright © 1998 by Abdo Consulting Group, Inc., Pentagon Tower, P.O. Box 36036, Minneapolis, Minnesota 55435 USA. International copyrights reserved in all countries. No part of this book may be reproduced in any form without written permission from the publisher.

Printed in the United States.

Cover and Interior Photo credits: Duomo
                                            Allsports
                                            Sports Illustrated

Edited by Kal Gronvall

Library of Congress Cataloging-in-Publication Data

Joseph, Paul, 1970-
Tiger Woods / by Paul Joseph.
      p.   cm.--(Awesome athletes)
Includes index.
Summary: Examines the life and accomplishments of the young, racially mixed golfer who destroyed his competition in his first major pro tournament, The Masters, and broke records that had stood for many years.
ISBN 1-56239-841-5
1. Woods, Tiger--Juvenile literature. 2. Golfers--United States--Biography--Juvenile literature.
[1. Woods, Tiger. 2. Golfers. 3. Racially mixed people--Biography.] I. Title. II. Series.
GV964.W66J67 1998
796.352'092
[B]--DC21
                                                            97-24866
                                                             CIP
                                                                 AC

Contents

The Master of Golf

No one in the game of golf has added as much excitement and fanfare as Tiger Woods has. In fact, many people feel that golf is boring and is only played by old men. But all that changed when Tiger Woods came along. Woods, the 21-year-old African, Asian, and Native American, has made the game cool for everyone.

Tiger began playing golf when he was still wearing diapers. His father sawed off a putter and gave him the small club. At a very young age Tiger began entering tournaments and even won them. By the time he was 14, Tiger had won five junior world titles—more junior titles than any other golfer in history!

When he was just 16, Tiger qualified to play in a Professional Golf Association (PGA) tournament. He was the youngest golfer ever to play in a PGA tour event.

After winning three U.S. **Amateur** titles in a row, Tiger became a professional (**pro**) and joined the PGA. He took the PGA by storm.

4

In his first tournament as a **pro** he took first place. And in his first major tournament as a pro—The Masters—he destroyed all the competition. It was an unbelievable feat. He not only won the Masters but he also broke **records** that had stood for many years.

At only 21, it is safe to say that Tiger Woods is one of the greatest golfers in the history of the game. He got there, however, by working hard, fighting the odds, and believing in himself. Tiger is truly the master of golf.

Tiger Woods sinks a putt at the Masters.

The Little Kitten

Eldrick "Tiger" Woods grew up in a middle-class family in Cypress, California, just outside of Los Angeles. His mother, Kultida, was from Thailand. His father, Earl, an African American, was an American soldier in the army. The two met when Earl served in Vietnam. In 1975, they had a son and named him Eldrick. His father nicknamed his son, "Tiger," after a friend he had served with in Vietnam.

His father believed that Tiger was going to be a great golfer—even as a baby. His father would practice hitting a golf ball into a net in the family's garage. From his high chair, six-month-old Tiger watched him. When Tiger was just under a year old, his father sawed off a golf club and gave it to him. Tiger could swing the club exactly like his father!

At the age of two, Tiger was already making waves with his unbelievable golf game. Tiger was even on the local television news showing off his golf swing. When he was three years old, he was on a show with entertainer Bob Hope. He amazed the television audience by driving a golf ball farther than Hope—who was an avid golfer!

Tiger loved the game of golf. As a four year old he begged his parents to take him to the golf **course**. On Saturdays he would go to the course at 9 a.m. and stay until 5 p.m., just hitting balls. Crowds of people would sit and watch this amazing child. Tiger would get upset when his father would tell him he had to stop and eat lunch, or worse yet, leave.

When Tiger was five years old he was on the nationally broadcast television show "That's Incredible." Tiger stunned the crowd with his golf swing. One person joked that he thought he was watching the famous golfer Jack Nicklaus shrunk to 50 pounds! After the show, a man asked for Tiger's **autograph**. Tiger didn't know how to sign his name so he printed it instead. The man said, "Thanks, and I will see you on the [PGA] tour some day." Tiger didn't quite understand. His father, however, just smiled.

Already Making History

Although Tiger would practice golf for hours on end, his parents taught him that other things were important too. Tiger's mother and father encouraged him to practice golf but never pushed him. They did make sure that his school work and chores came before anything else—including golf. Tiger also knew the importance of other activities. He was excellent in school, and at only 13 years old knew that he wanted to go to Stanford University for college.

As a youngster, Tiger's father often served as his **caddie**, carrying his clubs and giving him advice on the **course**. His mother went to most of his tournaments and was his number one fan. Both parents celebrated with him when he won and tried to console him when he lost—which wasn't often.

By the time Tiger was 14, he had won five Junior World Tournaments, which is more tournament victories than any other golfer in the history of the game. He also won many lesser known tournaments bringing home more than 100 golf trophies. Tiger was getting so good that he began beating professionals—still at only 14! In August, 1990, Tiger played against 21 **pros** in a tournament. He beat or tied all but three of them!

When Tiger was 16, he qualified to play in a PGA tournament—the Los Angeles Open. He was the youngest golfer ever to play in a PGA event. To Tiger, it was just another tournament. To everyone else, Tiger was truly amazing.

Young Tiger Woods practicing in Cypress, California.

Fighting The Odds

When Tiger was playing against the **course**, he never had a problem. When Tiger was playing against a professional 20 years older than he was, he never got nervous. When Tiger played in his first Masters tournament in 1995, he referred to it as "just another tournament." The only enemy that Tiger had to beat on the course each day was **racism**.

Tiger is very proud of his heritage. Sometimes he calls himself Asian American, and other times an African American, but generally he likes to be referred to as just an American. He doesn't want to be the best black golfer ever, he wants to be the best golfer ever.

Many people, however, refer to him as a black golfer. Tiger is one of only a few African Americans to become a **pro** golfer. One reason that so few African Americans play golf is that many private golf courses didn't allow blacks to play on their course. Even today, there are clubs that don't allow African Americans to play.

The golf course that hosted the Masters for many years did not allow black golfers to play on their **course**. The Masters' founder, Clifford Roberts, once said, "As long as I'm alive, golfers will be white, and **caddies** will be black."

Tiger's parents spent many nights drying the tears of their eight-year-old son who had nightmares about being killed while playing on a golf course in the South.

In Tiger's first PGA tournament when he was only 16, the head of the tournament received frightening phone calls about a black person playing in the tournament. One was even a death threat to Tiger. Tiger was very brave and decided to play despite the threats.

Before his first tournament in college, Tiger received a **racist** and threatening letter. Again Tiger didn't get discouraged. He taped the nasty message to his wall and decided to fight the racism on the golf course.

A day before he was to play in his first Masters, Tiger received many threatening letters. When Tiger sees something like this he is always reminded of what his mother said many years before. "Racism is not your problem, it's theirs."

It's very sad when a young person must go through so much to play a game he loves. But Tiger proved to **racists** that words will not stop him. He has also shown young people that they can do or be anything they want, no matter what anyone says.

Tiger had to battle more than just the golf course.

Off to Stanford

When Tiger was just 13 years old, he wrote a letter to Stanford University, saying how much he wanted to go to their college. He told them that he wanted to study business and be on their golf team.

Tiger worked and studied very hard and was an honor student in high school. He won a national award for being one of the best student athletes in the country.

In 1994, Tiger graduated from Western High School in Anaheim, California, and earned a full **scholarship** to study at Stanford. As a freshman in college, Tiger was one of the most popular athletes on campus.

His teammates loved to watch Tiger practice golf. Tiger could make the hardest of shots look easy. The best part was when Tiger would announce, "It's D time, fellas," which meant driver time. Woods would pull out his driver and hit some of the longest balls that his teammates had ever seen.

Tiger is well known for his driving power.

1975	**1991**	**1994**	**1995**
Born in Cypress, CA.	Played in Los Angeles Open, first PGA tournament.	Attended Stanford University.	Played in his first Masters Tournament.

How Awesome Is He?

Here is a list of U.S. Amateur Title winners and their ages.

Golfer	Year	Age
Tiger Woods	**1994**	**18**
Jack Nicklaus	1959	19
Robert Gardner	1909	19
Louis James	1902	19
Bruce Fleisher	1968	19
Nathaniel Crosby	1981	19

TIGER WOODS

AGE: 21
HEIGHT: 6 feet 2 inches
WEIGHT: 150 pounds

1995

Became millionaire signing contracts with NIKE and TITLEIST.

1997

Named Sports Illustrated Sportsman of the Year.

1997

Set up Tiger Woods Foundation for College scholarships.

1997

Won first Masters Tournament.

- **1997 Sports Illustrated Sportsman of the Year.**
- **Appeared on television show "That's Incredible" at age five.**
- **Youngest player to compete in a PGA tournament.**
- **Played golf for Stanford University beginning in 1994.**
- **Won his first Masters Tournament in 1997.**

Highlights

A teammate remembers one day when Tiger, who was carrying his driver in his right hand, was about 60 yards away at the other end of the driving range. The teammate punched a shot at Tiger. As Tiger walked toward the quickly moving ball he grabbed his driver with his other hand and took a full swing while still walking, and while the ball was still rolling. The teammate said the ball went about 290 yards—perfectly straight! "It is the most impressive shot I have ever seen or will ever see," said the teammate.

At Stanford, Tiger settled into the routine of school. Although the school work was very difficult and time consuming, he still maintained excellent grades while becoming the best **amateur** golfer in the world.

Tiger helped Stanford win many tournaments, but as an individual golfer he was awesome. In the 1994 U.S. Amateur Golf Tournament, Tiger came from behind to win the title as the best amateur golfer in the country. He also made history, becoming the youngest person to ever win the title at only 18 years old. He also became the first African American ever to win the tournament.

**Tiger Woods at
Stanford in 1994**

The Masters

At only 18, Tiger was easily the greatest **amateur** golfer in the world. People couldn't wait until he turned **pro** to see how he would do on the PGA Tour. Tiger, however, was determined to stay in school, play golf for Stanford, keep his amateur status, and then turn pro.

Because Tiger was the 1994 U.S. Amateur Champion, he was invited to the 1995 Masters. The Masters, in Augusta, Georgia, is one of the four major professional golf tournaments in the world (the U.S. Open, the British Open, and the PGA Championship are the others).

The Masters has a long tradition, and the best professional golfers compete for the tournament's top prize—the green jacket. The Masters didn't allow an African American to play in their tournament until 1975. Tiger would be only the fourth African American to compete.

Tiger was very excited to play in one of the greatest golf tournaments. For five months leading up to the tournament, Tiger began studying the family collection of videos of previous Masters tournaments.

In April, when he arrived at the tournament, he was mobbed by the media. They wanted to see this young African-American golfer. Tiger, however, downplayed the excitement, calling this event, "just another tournament."

Rain was coming down hard the morning of the first round of the Masters. But that didn't take away from the thrill of the crowd that was huddled around the first **tee box** waiting for Tiger's turn. When Tiger stepped to the tee box the crowd was down right giddy—they knew that they were seeing the beginning of a new era of golf.

Tiger played the first round with defending Masters champion Jose Maria Olazabal. The two were followed all day by a huge **gallery**—in the rain! After the round ended, Tiger had shot a **par**-72, six shots behind the leader. Although he wasn't leading, the fans and the other players watched his game in total amazement. On the 500-yard 15th hole, Woods hit a 340-yard **drive**. It was the longest of the day. "I had to watch his shots with binoculars," joked Olazabal.

After the second day, Woods was the only **amateur** to make the cut. He finished the tournament in 42nd place, ahead of such greats as Jack Nicklaus, U.S. Open champion Payne Stewart, and PGA champion John Daly. Woods entered the most difficult tournament and fared very well. Many hoped he would turn **pro**, but Woods remained an amateur and went back to Stanford.

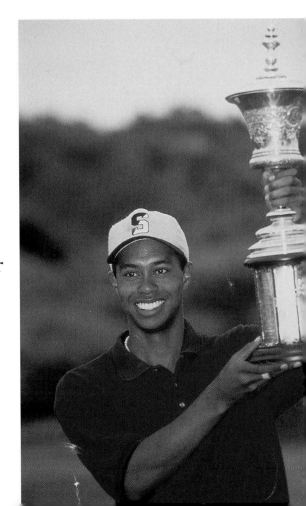

Tiger Woods winning the U.S. Amateurs Championship in 1995.

Turning Pro

Tiger played as an **amateur** for two more years, picking up two more U.S. Amateur Championships for a total of three in a row—the most ever in the history of golf.

Then the time came when Tiger gave up his amateur status and headed to the PGA Tour. On the day he announced he would turn **pro**, Tiger signed a five-year, $40 million contract with Nike—the most ever for an athlete. He also signed a multi-million dollar contract with Titleist. Tiger had yet to play as a professional but was already a millionaire—at only 20 years old.

Tiger, however, wasn't satisfied with just the money. He wanted to become the greatest golfer to ever play the game. Tiger charged out of the gate in his first tournament as a pro—the Mercedes Championships. He blew away the competition with a 14 under **par**, and on the last day he **recorded** an amazing seven under par-65.

In Tiger's next five tournaments he grabbed four top-20 finishes, including second place at the Pebble Beach National Pro-Am Tournament. Up to that point Tiger had played 27 rounds as a **pro**. Seventeen of those rounds were under **par**, with 10 being in the 60s! Tiger had earned nearly a half million dollars—in only his first six tournaments.

As a professional, Tiger was taking the world by storm. Sports Illustrated named him Sportsman of the Year. But people hadn't seen anything yet. Tiger was just getting started. During a weekend in April, of 1997, Tiger changed golf forever.

Tiger hitting an approach shot.

Tiger Gets A Green Jacket

Tiger was getting ready to play in his third Masters tournament. However, it was the first time as a **pro**. It was an incredible sight. People just wanted to catch a glimpse of this young, **phenomenal** golfer. Everyone knew that he had the talent to win a tournament—he had already done it. But could he win a major with cameras and crowds of people from all around the world watching his every move? Many believed it was too much **pressure** for such a young man.

After the first nine holes it seemed that the pressure was too much. He shot a four-over 40. Then the typical Tiger came alive. He shot an unbelievable 30 on the back nine and never looked back. The next three rounds were 66, 65, 69, for an amazing 18-under **par**, and an unheard of 12-**stroke** victory.

As Tiger walked up the last hole he knew he had just captured his childhood dream—winning the Masters. The fans were screaming his name and Tiger smiled and waved his hat. After sinking the final putt he walked over to his parents and gave his father and mother long hugs. The Masters' victory was a result of years of hard work by a very close family.

Tiger at age 15 with his parents Earl and Kultida Woods.

Tiger gets his green jacket after winning The Masters Tournament.

A Cool Cat

Tiger's performance in the Masters was the most outstanding in golf history. And he did it with the most **pressure** ever put on a golfer. People watched his every move. They watched because he was black in a world of white golfers and white crowds. They watched because of his youth in a game where players averaged 38 years old. They watched because of his unbelievable drives—323 yards on average, 25 yards longer than the next player. They watched because they wanted to see if this kid would ever fold under pressure. They watched because he was Tiger, and he was about to make golf history.

For winning the tournament Tiger received the prized green jacket. As he put it on he smiled, knowing that he had accomplished his dream through hard work, overcoming some of the major obstacles in his life. His father looked at Tiger with his green jacket on and said, "Green and black go well together, don't they?"

Giving Back

Although Tiger has worked very hard to get where he is, he also knows that he is very lucky. Tiger wants to give something back to the sport, to the fans, and especially to the young kids who never had a chance like Tiger did.

Tiger has always wanted to give something back to the less fortunate. When he was only seven years old he watched the scenes of children starving in Ethiopia (a country in Africa) on the evening news. He went right to his bedroom, opened his piggy bank, and took out 20 dollars. He asked his father to send it to them.

As a college student, Tiger would invite busloads of inner-city kids to the golf **course**, and Tiger would talk to them and teach them about the game of golf. He would also talk about the dangers of drugs and alcohol, but he would do it in a very entertaining way. He would say, "Here is Tiger on drugs," and Tiger would stagger to the

Tiger Woods at the 1997 Mercedes Championships.

tee box, topping the ball so it bounced crazily to the side. And then he would say, "Here is Tiger *not* on drugs," and presto, he would launch a 350-yard rocket across the sky.

Tiger would also talk about respect, trust, and hard work. He would encourage kids to work hard and go after their dreams. He told them they didn't have to be golfers or athletes. No matter what they wanted to be he would always say that it would never happen if they didn't work hard in school, respect their parents and teachers, and stay off drugs.

Tiger continued to give back whenever he could. It was around 6 p.m., after the second round of his first Masters tournament. Tiger was very tired but he still took a ride over to a public golf **course** about 10 miles away to meet with all of the black **caddies** from Augusta National. After that he gave a golf clinic to a group of black children. Tiger was having fun, and the children were laughing and smiling. They could sense that someone special cared about them.

As a **pro**, Tiger continues to give back. He has set up the Tiger Woods Foundation that funds college **scholarships** across the country for underprivileged children. This foundation also sets up clinics, hires golf coaches, and funds golf **courses** for inner-city children.

Tiger knows how lucky he is and knows that children

look up to him. He wants to do this, loves to do this, but most of all believes he must do this. Tiger explained, "my dad has always taught me these words: care and share."

Tiger Woods has brightened the game of golf unlike no other.

Glossary

Amateur - An Athlete who does not get paid for playing sports.

Autograph - A person's name written in his or her handwriting.

Caddie - A person who helps a golfer by carrying his or her clubs.

Course - The land on which people play golf.

Drive - To hit a golf ball off the tee box with a driver.

Driver - The club a golfer uses off the tee box.

Gallery - The people who watch golf tournaments in person.

Par - The score standard set for each hole.

Phenomenal - A very talented person—almost unbelievable.

Pro - (Professional) Someone who makes money playing golf.

Pressure - Putting too many expectations on yourself and feeling stress.

Racism - To treat people unfairly because of the color of their skin or because of their beliefs.

Record - The best it has ever been done in a certain event.

Scholarship - Money given to a student to attend a school because of their athletic or academic ability.

Stroke - One shot in a golf match.

Tee Box - The place where golfers begin playing a hole.

PASS IT ON

Tell Others Something Special About Your Favorite Sports or Athletes

What makes your favorite athlete awesome? Do you think you have a chance to be an Awesome Athlete? Tell us about your favorite plays, tournaments, and anything else that has to do with sports. We want to hear from you!

To get posted on ABDO & Daughters website E-mail us at "sports@abdopub.com"

Index